Carnival

by Grace Hansen

Abdo
WORLD FESTIVALS
Kids

Abdo Kids Jumbo is an Imprint of Abdo Kids
abdobooks.com

abdobooks.com

Published by Abdo Kids, a division of ABDO, P.O. Box 398166, Minneapolis, Minnesota 55439. Copyright © 2023 by Abdo Consulting Group, Inc. International copyrights reserved in all countries. No part of this book may be reproduced in any form without written permission from the publisher. Abdo Kids Jumbo™ is a trademark and logo of Abdo Kids.

Printed in the United States of America, North Mankato, Minnesota.

102022
012023

THIS BOOK CONTAINS RECYCLED MATERIALS

Photo Credits: Alamy, Getty Images, Shutterstock PREMIER, ©Prof. Mortel p.6/ CC BY 2.0, ©Egisto Sani p.7/ CC BY-NC-SA 2.0

Production Contributors: Teddy Borth, Jennie Forsberg, Grace Hansen
Design Contributors: Candice Keimig, Pakou Moua

Library of Congress Control Number: 2021950542
Publisher's Cataloging-in-Publication Data

Names: Hansen, Grace, author.
Title: Carnival / by Grace Hansen.
Description: Minneapolis, Minnesota : Abdo Kids, 2023 | Series: World festivals | Includes online resources and index.
Identifiers: ISBN 9781098261740 (lib. bdg.) | ISBN 9781098262587 (ebook) | ISBN 9781098263003 (Read-to-Me ebook)
Subjects: LCSH: Carnival--Juvenile literature. | Mardi Gras (Festival)--Juvenile literature. | Festivals--Juvenile literature. | Manners and customs--Juvenile literature.
Classification: DDC 394.2683--dc23

Table of Contents

A Joyful Event 4

History of Carnival 6

Carnival Today 16

Carnival Around the World 22

Glossary 23

Index 24

Abdo Kids Code 24

A Joyful Event

Carnival is a joyful event that takes place each year. It is celebrated by countries and **cultures** around the world.

History of Carnival

Carnival and events like it have been enjoyed for centuries. Long ago, the ancient Greeks came together to celebrate the end of winter. They honored Dionysus, the god of vegetation and fertility.

Dionysus

The springtime celebration later spread to the Romans in Italy. There, the first pre-Lent Carnivals took place. Lent is the 40 days before Easter in the Christian calendar.

The festival's name likely comes from the Latin language. *Carne vale* means "farewell to meat." Christians **fasted** and did not eat meat during Lent. People today give up other foods too, like sweet treats.

The Fight Between Carnival and Lent painting

Early Carnivals in Italy were celebrated with masked balls. There was music and dancing. Everyone enjoyed their favorite things to eat and drink before the start of Lent.

Carnival spread throughout Europe and then to the Americas. The Portuguese brought the celebration to Brazil. Brazil is a melting pot of many **cultures**, including some from Africa.

Carnival Today

Carnival in Rio de Janeiro, Brazil, is an exciting event. It has strong African influences. The masks and costumes are bright and flashy. **Samba** dancing is everywhere.

Each day of the celebration, about two million people fill the streets of Rio. The **samba school** parade is a highlight for many. Each school has a giant float and colorful costumes.

In the United States, Carnival is called Mardi Gras. *Mardi Gras* means "Fat Tuesday" in French. French explorers first celebrated it on March 3, 1699, near present-day New Orleans, Louisiana. It is a holiday many look forward to each year.

Carnival Around the World

Einsiedeln, Switzerland
- A unique celebration with devil masks, pitchforks, and the loud clanging of bells
- Meant to drive out evil spirits and welcome spring

Mazatlán, Mexico
- While Carnival is celebrated in more than 200 cities in Mexico, Mazatlán's is the largest
- Known for its amazing fireworks displays and live music

Port of Spain, Trinidad & Tobago
- The largest Carnival celebration in the Caribbean
- Lasts for months, but the final 3 days are the most exciting
- Known for steel pan competitions and unique costumes

Venice, Italy
- Celebrated since 1162
- Famous for its revelers wearing Venetian masks, which can be made from leather, porcelain, or glass

Glossary

century – a period of time of 100 years.

culture – the language, customs, ideas, and art of a particular group of people.

fast – to eat no food.

fertility – the ability to produce farm crops or other plant life.

samba – a ballroom dance, or music for this dance from Brazil. Samba has a complex mix of influences. Its origins are mainly from African cultures.

samba school – dancing, marching, and drumming clubs that have a strong community basis and are traditionally associated with a particular neighborhood in Brazil.

Index

Africa 14, 16
ancient Greeks 6
ancient Romans 8
Brazil 14, 16, 18
costumes 18
dancing 12, 16
Dionysus (Greek god) 6

Easter 8
France 20
Greece 6
Italy 8, 12
Latin 10
Lent 8, 10, 12
Mardi Gras 20

Portugal 14
samba 16
samba school parade 18
spring 4, 8, 20
United States 20

Visit **abdokids.com** to access crafts, games, videos, and more!

Use Abdo Kids code **WCK1740** or scan this QR code!